THE NISM BOOK

ZEPHYR O'ZOLOCHI

ISBN 979-8-89043-069-4 (paperback)
ISBN 979-8-89043-070-0 (digital)

Christian Faith Publishing
832 Park Avenue
Meadville, PA 16335
www.christianfaithpublishing.com

Printed in the United States of America

Contents

Preface

I offer you an explanation of the symbol in the center of the front cover of this book: it is an Egyptian reed leaf hieroglyph which is the main symbol of Nism. It is the main symbol of Nism because it inspired me to create the Reed Leaf Sun (the rays and eyes of the sun are made from the hieroglyph); therefore, it represents light. As the founder of Nism, that is my choice.

The Reed Leaf Sun

The Ten Commandments of Nism

1. You must know that N is a name of God.
2. You must know that N most deeply loves humanity.
3. You must know that Nism is the name of this religion.
4. You must know that Nism is followed by an Nist.
5. You must answer this question: Are you an Nist?
6. You must know that angels are a species, just like humans are a species.
7. You must know that relations between angels and humans are acrointerspecificity.
8. You must know that N is lupraacrointerspecific (God transcends relations between angels and humans).
9. You must know that in Nism jurisprudence, N has lupraacrointerspecific ecclesiastical jurisdiction over all churches.
10. All individuals deserve to have their own official personal coat of arms and personal

flag, which must be designed and provided for them by a government.

Notes: *Nism* is pronounced "en-ism." The word *Nism* is formed from the name of God—N, together with the suffix *-ism*. *Nist* is pronounced "en-ist." The Ten Commandments of Nism are the legal successors of the biblical Ten Commandments. The prefix *acro-* means "high." *Acrointerspecificity* is high interspecificity. *Interspecificity* is something that occurs between members of different species. *Acrointerspecificity* is something that occurs between members of different *highly intelligent* species (primarily referring to humans and angels, but this also includes aliens) (e.g., a frog eating a fly is low interspecificity, not acro-interspecificity). The prefix of *lupra-* means "transcends" from Latin *supra-*, describing N as lupraacrointerspecific is distinct. I think commandments 1 to 8 are easy to understand, commandment 9 is a tad hard to understand, and commandment 10 is a gift. Coats of arms are not just for royalty, nobility, clergy, presidents, countries, and corporations; all individuals deserve to have their own official personal coat of arms.

My Seal, Coat of Arms, and Flag

My seal

My coat of arms

My flag

My seal contains the Reed Leaf Sun, and so does my coat of arms, along with some fun decorations. My flag has an Egyptian feather hieroglyph in the center, which is surrounded by stars, shapes, a hashtag, the seal of Prophet Muhammad, a crown, and the OM symbol—all for prettiness. The background of my flag is white with scattered gold thread decoration, and there is a white border.

Your Coat of Arms and Flag

At the time of writing, the vast majority of people do not have their own official personal coat of arms and flag designed and provided for them by a government.

Perhaps you are from a noble family and already have your own official personal coat of arms and personal flag, but the vast majority of people do not. Drawing from the tenth commandment of Nism, I want the arms less and flagless to think about what your personal coat of arms and flag might look like. What design might you come up with in cooperation with a government? Would you create your own symbol as I did with the Reed Leaf Sun and have that placed on your arms? What is your favorite color? Would you use your favorite color on your flag?

When you have a coat of arms, you can place it at the top of the letters that you write, you can place it at the top of your curriculum vitae, and you can use it as decoration in your home. Those are just a few ideas.

One reason why it is right for governments to provide and design personal coats of arms for all individuals is that having your personal coat of arms gives you an artistic, physical, and systematic symbol of your identity that has a calming effect on the mind. It makes you feel valued, connected to reality, and connected to history, likewise with your own flag.

Archangel Gabriel Visited Me

In June 2010, when I was nineteen years old, a male angel visited me. I believe that this angel was Archangel Gabriel due to the air of stern authority that I sensed. I do not remember the exact date, but I cite the eleventh of June 2010 at around 1800 hours as the most likely.

His Illuminating Youthful Ancientness Archangel Gabriel (who is of a species separate from humans) visited me in person (not in a dream) in June 2010 at my grandfather David's house, 17 Longford Road, Bognor Regis, Sussex, England, PO21 1AA.

I was lying on my bed, relaxing, when Archangel Gabriel arrived in my bedroom in a tiny UFO. His UFO is a tiny black orb that is approximately fifteen millimeters in diameter. The black orb must have traveled through the walls with invisibility until it made itself known to me. When the tiny black orb was stationary midair in front of me, it then opened up into a large circular portal of approximately one and a half meters in diameter. Inside the portal were mist and clouds.

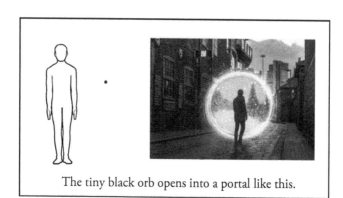

The tiny black orb opens into a portal like this.

Archangel Gabriel then appeared through the mist and clouds and came to the front of the portal to greet me. Archangel Gabriel's height appeared as about six feet one, and he had light-honey-brown shoulder-length hair, an athletic build (a mesomorph frame), a perfectly beautiful face, Caucasian-colored skin, and very large mesmerizing wings made of very ancient-looking light-cream-colored feathers. He was wearing a white buttoned-up long-sleeve shirt with black trousers, and he appeared as being about thirty-five years old (in human years). He was standing upright with brilliant posture, and he elegantly extended his left arm out to greet me; he extended his left arm through the portal and into my room. Then, spontaneously, a bright green light began emitting from my belly button. The bright green light took the form of an umbilical cord as it slowly protruded from my body. The bright green light then wrapped itself around Archangel Gabriel's left hand as a greeting. The bright green light then unwrapped from Gabriel's left hand, and it slowly made its way back into my body (this production of light is scientifically known as bioluminescence). Then Gabriel drew his left arm back inside the portal, and the portal with Archangel Gabriel still inside quickly closed back into the tiny black orb UFO and disappeared. A gentle wave of deep peace then flowed through my body.

This was the one and only time I have seen Archangel Gabriel and his UFO. At the time, I told my friends and family about it, and from around 2020 onward, I informed different branches of the UK government about it, such as the British Army, MI5, and the Civil Aviation Authority. I have also informed the US Central Intelligence Agency about it as well as the United States Army. In addition, between autumn 2022 and January 2023, I informed these organizations about the visit:

- The International Civil Aviation Organization

- The Royal Aeronautical Society
- The Fairy Investigation Society
- Yale Divinity School
- Harvard Divinity School
- The Church of England Parliamentary Office
- The House of Commons Ecclesiastical Committee (UK)
- The House of Commons Science and Technology Committee (UK)
- The Modern Fairy Sightings Podcast
- The Department of Religious Studies at New York University
- The Faculty of Divinity at Cambridge University
- The School of Divinity at the University of St Andrews
- The Department of Theology and Religious Studies at the University of San Diego
- The Department of Religious Studies at Brown University
- The Third Committee of the United Nations General Assembly

I informed the US and UK governments and those different organizations about it because I wanted to spread the good news, hear opinions, and build up my confidence.

I believe that the 2010 visit from Archangel Gabriel was the beginning of my ordination as the Pharaoh (supreme leader) of the Nism Church and as the Nism Bishop of Sussex.

Here are some of the responses I have received so far about my Archangel Gabriel story:

I received this response via email from the Dean of Yale Divinity School (gregory.sterling@yale.edu):

> *Dear Zephyr,*
>
> *Sounds like you had a powerful experience, whether subjective or objective.*
>
> *Sincerely,*
> *Greg Sterling*

I received this response via email from the Royal Aeronautical Society (communications@aerosociety.com):

> *Dear Zephyr,*
>
> > *Thanks for your correspondence. Unfortunately, this activity is outside of our remit so [we] are not able to comment on the report.*
> >
> > *Kind regards,*
> > *Rebecca Thi*
> > *Communications and*
> > *Content Manager*
> > *Royal Aeronautical Society*

I received this response via email from the director of operations of the School of Divinity at the University of St. Andrews (divdop@st-andrews.ac.uk):

> *Dear Zephyr O'Zolochi,*
>
> > *I acknowledge receipt of your email to the School of Divinity,*

dated 29 October 2022. The alleged matters do not fall within the jurisdiction of the School of Divinity. I am unable to correspond further on this topic.

Yours sincerely,
Dr. Eric Stoddart (he/his)
Director of Operations
St. Mary's College,
School of Divinity
University of St Andrews,
Fife, Scotland KY16 9JU

I received this response via email from the United States Army's Dyess Air Force Base in Texas (7CS.Dyess.FOIA@us.af.mil):

HAHAHAHAHAHAHAHAHAHA-
HAHAHAHAHAHAHAHAHAHAHAHAHA-
HAHAHAHAHAHAHAHAHAHAHAHAHA-
HAHAHAHAHAHAHAHAHAHAHAHHA-
HAHAHAHAHAHAHAHAHAHA
HAHAHAHAHAHAHAHAHAHA-
HAHAHAHAHAHAHAHAHAHAHAHAHA-
HAHAHHAHAHAHAHAHAHAHAHAHA-

HAHAHAHAHAHAHAHAHAHAHAHAHA-
HAHAHAHAHAHAHAHAHAHAHAHAHA-
HAHA

I received this response via email from the UK Civil Aviation Authority (richard.taylor@caa.co.uk):

> *Zephyr*
>
> *With respect, we have no legal duty to investigate UFO reports.*
>
> *Kind regards*
> *Richard Taylor*
> *Communications Department*
> *Civil Aviation Authority*

I received this response via email from the House of Commons Science and Technology Committee (scitechcom@parliament.uk):

> *Dear Zephyr,*
>
> *Thank you for your e-mail and letters to the Science and*

Technology Committee. This has been passed to me for response.

I'm afraid the matters you raise do not fall within the remit of the Committee and therefore the Committee is unable to launch an inquiry. Thank you for taking the time to get in touch.

Thanks,
Danielle Nash

I received this response via email from the Department of Theology and Religious Studies at the University of San Diego (fuller@sandiego.edu):

Dear Zephyr O'Zolochi,

My apologies for the delay in responding to your email. I am afraid that like others you have corresponded with, this is not our area of expertise or jurisdiction. I wish you well in your quest to bring this to the attention of the proper human authorities. with best wishes,

> *Dr. Russell E. Fuller*
> *Professor of Hebrew*
> *Bible and Chair*
> *Department of Theology*
> *and Religious Studies*

I received this response via email from the Department of Religious Studies at Brown University (Religious_Studies@brown.edu):

Dear Zephyr,

> *Please forgive the delayed reply. I'm afraid this is outside our area of expertise. We wish you the best of luck with your pursuits.*

> *Religious Studies Department,*
> *Brown University*
> *Box 1927, The Shirley Miller*
> *House, 59 George Street,*
> *Providence, RI 02912*

I would like to share one further email that I have received; however, this email was regarding a copy of the Nism Church Charter that I sent. The email is from the Anglican Bishop of Rajasthan (North India), the Right Reverend Darbara Singh (darbarasingh0145@gmail.com):

Subject: Re: Nism Church Charter

Praise The Lord
Received your email
Thanks
May God Bless the NISM church

From,
Darbara Singh
9079255282

Jesus Christ Visited Me

In February 2009, when I was aged eighteen, I arrived in Sydney, Australia, for several months of traveling. In June 2009, I arrived in Darwin, the capital city of Australia's Northern Territory, with my Dutch friend Deidre Douma and our rented car. After settling into our accommodation in Darwin, I decided I wanted to visit a local spiritual healer. I then booked an appointment for a healing session and attended. I do not remember the exact date, but I cite the twelfth of June 2009 at around 1400 hours as being the most likely. The spiritual healer was female, but I don't remember her name or the name of her business. After an introductory chat, I lay down on the therapy bed, closed my eyes, and she began a guided meditation with her hands on my shoulders. Suddenly I entered a higher level of consciousness, a great sense of peace came over me, and the room changed. The room turned into a very dimly lit heavenly state, and all the furniture disappeared apart from the therapy bed, and the female spiritual healer had disappeared too, and I could no longer hear her soothing voice. I was peacefully staring into the blackness when Jesus Christ appeared in the room; he slowly emerged from the blackness. Jesus Christ was standing, wearing a white robe, and white light was emanating from his body. He had a golden halo above his head, his skin was tan, and his hands were together in the praying position. He was looking at me with a smile on his most beautiful face, and he was praying. He was looking at me while praying, which lasted for about two minutes, then I felt a tapping on my shoulder, and I returned to normal awareness. Jesus Christ disappeared, the room turned back into how it was before, and the female spiritual healer stopped tapping on my shoulder, and she said that she thought I had fallen asleep. I didn't explain to her what happened, and the session came to an end. I then returned to my accommodation.

I believe that this experience was the official Second Coming of Jesus Christ. I would also like you to know that around 2014, my grandmother Lesley told me that Jesus Christ and two angels had visited her via a ladder made of light.

So now that the official Second Coming of Jesus Christ has been received, what is the next main event? Building Nism is what is next. I believe that Christianity is evolving into Nism, and so are many other religions. Buddhism is evolving into Nism.

Hinduism is evolving into Nism. Islam is evolving into Nism. I am guiding this process.

Here are the main goals when you follow Nism:

- To live in harmony with N as much as possible.
- To worship N and all recognized deities regularly.
- To gather with other Nists regularly.
- To show obedience toward N.
- To not think about Nism all the time (have fun, don't be obsessive, and get good rest).
- To help gather reports of angel contact, fairy contact, and alien contact.
- To help celebrate those who have been contacted to encourage other contactees to come forward and to stimulate further contact.

Letter from the Office of the Roman Catholic Archbishop of Westminster

On the sixteenth of August 2022, I wrote via post to His Eminence, Cardinal Vincent Nichols, the Roman Catholic Archbishop of Westminster and president of the Catholic Bishops' Conference of England and Wales. I wrote to him regarding Her Majesty Queen Elizabeth II of the United Kingdom. His office replied to me via a post on the twentieth of August 2022. The envelope and letter that I received from his office are copied on the following two pages.

The letter helps Christianity evolve into Nism because it is a quite high-level official response from the Roman Catholic Church to the Nism Church.

Delivered by

Royal Mail

22-08-22
KO.51 P855T6G82

2
Letter

Zephyr O'Zolochi
Flat 5, Millfield Court
Courtwick Lane
Littlehampton
Sussex, BN17 7PA

ARCHBISHOP'S HOUSE,
WESTMINSTER. LONDON. SW1P 1QJ

Zephyr O'Zolochi
Flat 5, Millfield Court
Courtwick Lane
Littlehampton
Sussex, BN17 7PB

20 August 2022

Dear Mr O'Zolochi,

His Eminence Cardinal Vincent Nichols acknowledges receipt of your communication dated 16th August 2022.

As the Roman Catholic Archbishop of Westminster, the Cardinal does not have any connection with the Supreme Governor of the Church of England. Your communication is, therefore, returned herewith.

With kind regards,

The Office of His Eminence Cardinal Vincent Nichols
Archbishop's House I Ambrosden Avenue I London I SW1P 1QJ

Enc.

Some Advice for King Charles III

I find the book *Monas Hieroglyphica* by John Dee to be incredibly beautiful, reverent, and inspirational. I am particularly drawn to his inventiveness. John Dee was an Englishman who was born in London in 1527. He was an adviser of Queen Elizabeth I of England and Ireland, and it has been believed that William Shakespeare's character Prospero, a powerful wizard, was based on him.

I want to be like John Dee. I want to be an adviser to His Majesty King Charles III.

Along the lines of the Royal Victorian Order, I would advise King Charles to establish "The Most Healing Order of Charles III." This new order would partly be a response to the horrors of the transatlantic slave trade (i.e., descendants of slaves who currently have mental health difficulties could be inducted into the order). This would help to heal generational trauma and would show true sorrowfulness. In addition, it would be a rather grand example of innovative leadership.

Some Views of the Nism Church

View on creation

The Nism Church's view on creation is compatible with the big bang theory, the scientific age of the universe, the scientific age of the earth, and Darwin's theory of evolution.

View on monotheism and polytheism

The view is that at different times and in different situations, God, N, likes to be known differently. This means that N sometimes likes to be known as a singular deity, and at other times, N likes to be known as multiple deities. The Nism Church most keenly and officially worships Greek deities, Hindu deities, Shinto deities, ancient Egyptian deities, Maori deities, Chinese deities, Aztec deities, Roman deities, Celtic deities, and West African deities. This comes alongside the official worship of Jesus Christ, the Prophet Muhammad, Guru Nanak, and Gautama

Buddha, as well as others. Nism is both monotheistic and polytheistic.

View on homosexuality

The Nism Church does not discriminate against homosexuals. Homosexuality is normal.

View on Heaven

Heaven is an afterlife location, and good behavior ensures entry into heaven. Furthermore, the view is that different people experience heaven in different ways: God, N, likes to see individual people thinking about what heaven looks like to them; God, N, enjoys different interpretations of heaven. A person's relationship with heaven is personal—deeply personal.

For example, if you say that you believe the leader of heaven is a female Chinese dragon named Mong-Wu, then N *thoroughly* enjoys your view with you.

Nism leaders must *only provide this foundational idea of heaven*—individuals are to build their personal pictures of heaven upon the foundation provided.

View on one true church

The Nism Church does not consider itself to be the one true church. This is because the Nism Church believes that there are many highly intelligent alien species (extraterrestrials) who have their own valid and equivalent churches. Therefore, no church should claim to be the one true church. This is at odds with the Roman Catholic Church, which teaches that it is the one true church.

Reed Leaf Stars

Reed leaf stars are formed from the reed leaf hieroglyph, and they are important symbols within Nism.

Two Photographs of Me at Amberley Castle

My Successor

Who will be my successor as the Pharaoh of the Nism Church? Who will be my successor as the Nism Bishop of Sussex? Who will help to build the Nism Archdiocese of London? I want my successor to be an African American female who was born in the United States of America.

A List of Words to Study

Halo, Darwin, the Holy Spirit, Prada, *Rosicrucianism*, Cartier, *theistic evolution*, Valentino, Freemasonry, Gucci, liberal theology, Louis Vuitton, Meghan Markle, Givenchy, Rolls-Royce, Emilia Wickstead, time-related trinitarianism, Jenny Packham, Saudi Arabia, Dior, Jeep, Vivienne Westwood, drag queens, Versace, Ferrari, Chanel, Land Rover, Lamborghini, Maserati, Karl Lagerfeld, Armani, Miu Miu, Hermès, Jean Paul Gaultier, Yves Saint Laurent, Balmain, Roberto Cavalli, Burberry, Dolce & Gabbana, Viktor & Rolf, Bulgari, Ralph Lauren, Moschino, Carolina Herrera, Giuseppe Zanotti, Mouawad, Fendi, Fenty, Adidas, Nike, K-pop, Netflix, television, computers, smartphones, Microsoft, Google, Twitter, Bombardier, Airbus, cardinal beetles, Meryl Streep, Barack Obama, Michelle Obama, Disney, alchemical art, Vogue, the *globus cruciger*, freedom.

```
          HDTH
          SPCV
          FGLT
          LVM
MGREWTTJPSADJVWDQV
FCLRLMKLAMMHJPGYS
LBRCBD&GV&RBRLMCH
          GZM
          FFAN
          KNTC
          SMG
          TBA
          CBM
          SBO
          MOD
          AAVF
```

About the Author

The author wishes for you to know the meaning of his name. He has been using the name Zephyr O'Zolochi since early 2017, and he chose this name himself. Zephyr is a shortened version of Zephyrus, the name of a Greek wind god. He wanted to draw attention to a Greek wind god to help bridge together monotheism and polytheism. *O'Zolochi* means "golden halo" (the Celtic *O* being used as a halo and *Zolochi* formed from *Zoloto*, the Russian word for *gold*). He chose *O'Zolochi* because he thinks it's a clever reference to holiness.

He hopes that this book helps to heal you, comfort you, and inspire you.

Milton Keynes UK
Ingram Content Group UK Ltd.
UKHW020653151123
432602UK00010B/83

9 798890 430694